Back On Track To Financial Freedom

By

Andrew J. Green

This book is a work of non-fiction. Names and places have been changed to protect the privacy of all individuals. The events and situations are true.

ISBN: 1-4140-4953-6 (e-book)
ISBN: 1-4140-4952-8 (Paperback)

This book is printed on acid free paper.

1stBooks – rev. 01/07/04

Dedication

To my precious wife Krisi, who has stood by my side through the best and the worst of times. I love you. Also, to my high school English teacher, Lena O'Brien, and my college Professor of English, Dr. Ann Greco, who both encouraged me to write when I didn't want to. I thank you.

Table of Contents

Foreword

While traveling in Europe many years ago, I was a witness to a passenger train derailment in the mountains of southern Germany. The conductor had apparently lost control of the train while coming off of a steep grade and attempted to negotiate a sharp curve at a high rate of speed. The damage was incredible and the panic stricken passengers didn't know what to do.

Although many passengers had evacuated the damaged train, some were attempting to re-board it. They were in a state of shock to some degree and couldn't use rational judgment without help. Decisions that would seem to be common sense to a level headed person, were foreign to the frightened passengers involved in this incident. Eventually the area was cleared and the clean up crew moved the train to a station to be repaired. After several weeks, the mechanics repaired the train and had it back on the tracks in working order.

After reflecting on this experience, I can't help but find the similarities with the train derailment and the financial derailment people get themselves into everyday. Many people I talk to are out of control with their spending. They don't realize it until they try to negotiate a financial curve that their bank account can't handle. Eventually they become financially derailed. Just like the passengers on the train, they panic and make foolish decisions that could have been avoided if they had exercised common sense. But instead of making rational decisions, they are driven by fear and usually bury themselves up to their eyeballs in debt, not knowing what to do.

If you are one of the people I just described, RELAX!!! Because while you are reading this book, you will learn how to repair your financial situation. You will also learn how to keep control of your spending and learn how to invest, while still being able to enjoy life.

Introduction

I've spoken to some of the most intelligent people that anybody could meet. When the area of finances is brought up, many of these people haven't a clue to managing their finances. Most think they need to earn more money in order to get out of debt, but the old saying, "The more you make, the more you spend," couldn't be more accurate. When I met a man who earns over a million dollars a year and who just filed bankruptcy, I found that this man would never get out of debt as long as he couldn't control his spending. This man isn't alone. In fact, many people are having a hard time with their finances and with their debt, no matter how much money they earn. The following pages should help you to get control of your finances along with planning for your future.

I didn't write in all of the formulas and mathematical equations that tell you how financial plans work because that is not important. You don't need to know how a fuel injection system works, to drive a car or how a computers hard drive runs to use a computer. In the same way, you don't need to know how these plans work to use them. You can go to college and take up macro and microeconomics along with other financial courses and hope to learn half of what your about to read, but you don't need to. All you need to do is follow the plan that is in this book and let the plan do the work.

The Beast

Debt: To owe.

Andy's definition: A curse from Hell brought on by one's self, which once unleashed, will wreak havoc on one's life.

For years, people have asked me how to get out of debt and how to get ahead in life. Some are looking for a quick fix while others are looking for a permanent solution. The ability to getting out of debt and staying out lies somewhere between both of those desires. It's easy to get out of debt but it takes time. If it took someone 10 years to get into debt, than they shouldn't expect to resolve their debt situation in 6 months. People get all excited and fired up about getting out of debt quickly, only to become discouraged because they have set unrealistic goals and end up deeper in debt than they were before they went on their quest.

Getting out of debt and becoming debt free is a behavior that must be learned. Society has taught people to live on and to depend on credit in order to have something instead of owning what you buy. Society has taught us to earn good credit so that we can have that $200,000. house with a two stall garage, a new car in each stall, along with a new boat docked at the lake. What society didn't tell us is that we would be slaves to that dream, both husband and wife along with any children that come along.

The children suffer because Mom and Dad are out trying to pay for the American dream or trying to keep up with the Jones family instead of focusing on the most precious thing they have, and that is their family. Day Care and Latch Key Kids feel neglected but don't realize it because most of their friends are in the same shoes. Mom and Dad don't talk as much or have time for each other because they become consumed in their work and begin to grow apart. Before you know it, the marriage decays and separation becomes inevitable. So much for the American dream.

If people learned to manage their finances, they would have more time away from work to spend enjoying themselves, and that is what everyone really wants anyway. No one wants to become a divorced workaholic with an insurmountable amount of debt who dies at age 56 due to a heart attack or stroke as a result of work related stress.

Everyone works to have nice things and to feel successful while bringing home a paycheck. But, if you owe a debt on these "Things", you may work two to three times harder and longer to have these "Things". Because you must work longer, you have less time to enjoy the good things in life.

Could you imagine what it would be like to look forward to going to work instead of having to go to work? Imagine what it would be like to work twenty or thirty hours a week instead of fifty or sixty. Most of us, at one time, enjoyed our jobs because we chose the career we are in. But when wanting to do something becomes something you have to do, now this changes everything. You have to get control of finances or they will control you.

Credit is like a beast. If it can be controlled, than it can work well for you. But if it gets out of its cage, it will destroy your life and make living very miserable. Like fire, it can be a warming friend on a cold Winter's night, or it can become your worst nightmare when out of control. I want to help you control this beast called credit, otherwise your debt will rule over you, and it is a cruel taskmaster. For this to work, you are going to have to want it to work. You are going to have to lay aside your mind-sets and to discipline yourself to becoming financially and debt free.

The following chapters will help you to get control of your finances regardless of how wild they have become. I am going to show you a plan that has worked time and time again. You may find a different avenue that works, but the goal is to get out of debt no matter what road you take. Following through is the most important part of accomplishing your goals and not letting anything discourage you along the way. Don't quit once you have started because it will be difficult to restart again.

The Budget

A budget is basically a break down of all of your bills. The part that people need to learn is to discipline themselves to live by that budget. It's being accountable for every dollar that comes into your life.

Let's look at it like a company, and the company name is, "The Your Name Company". If you were the accountant for The Your Name Company, than you would be responsible for knowing exactly where every penny went concerning The Your Name Company. If money was mismanaged as a result of your actions, than you would be held personally responsible to The Your Name Company.

The first and foremost thing that must be done in order to know where your finances are being spent, is to make a list of all of your current bills and debts. Bills that would typically fall into this category would be anything that is considered an "everyday expense". For example: The phone bill, cellular phone bill, water, power, or heating bill, online service, groceries, homeowner's insurance, car insurance, gasoline for the car, rent or mortgage payment, and especially your miscellaneous spending account.

The reason I emphasize the miscellaneous account is because this can range from $20. a month to several hundreds of dollars a month. I've counseled people that have found that they spend well over a thousand dollars a month in this area alone. The miscellaneous area would include your entertainment costs, i.e. going out with your friends, ordering pizza or Chinese food, going to a concert, playing golf, eating fast food for lunch at work, or anything else that you spend money on that is not an actual necessity.

Included in your budget should be the "debt" you owe on credit cards, car loans, educational loans, boat and RV loans, or basically anything that will be reduced over a period of time. The reason I don't want you to include your home mortgage in this portion of the "debt" list is because I consider a home mortgage a long term loan that has a lower interest rate than the shorter term debts. Also, houses typically appreciate in value which I consider to be more of an investment than a common debt which depreciates in value as time goes on. An example of a budget list is on the last page of this chapter. This budget list is the single most important part of getting out of debt.

Most people that I counsel, don't have any idea as to where the money they earn every month goes to. As soon as they make this list, they typically find that they are wasting money on things they don't need, but purchase impulse items because the money is there at the time. Many confess that they don't know when their next bill is due, or what those bills are that will be due.

As soon as you finish your budget, add up all of your expenses together and deduct them from your take home pay. This will show you what you should have left over at the end of every month, on the average. I can almost guarantee that if you haven't been living by a budget, than you don't have the amount left over every month that you will find after deducting your expenses from your income.

For some people, this revelation of this new found money will be the first key to paying off debt and enjoying a better life. For others, you may find that your expenses exceed your income which simply means you have to tighten up the belt on your budget. The way to do this is to possibly see what expenses can be reduced. For example: Reduce your long distance phone bill by limiting the amount of calls you make. Limit the amount of time you spent on a call. If you contact your long distance carrier, you can purchase the 5 cent or 7 cent a minute contract that will only cost you around $4.95 every month. This $4.95 a month charge is typically added directly to your phone bill but may save you many times that amount every single month. Also, phone cards are wonderful and the least expensive way I've found to make long distance calls. My wife and I use a phone card exclusively because we only pay between 2 and 3 cents a minute and there are no connection or monthly fees to use the phone card as long as your not using a pay phone. Phone cards can be purchased at just about any retail store and when the minutes run out, you can call the customer service number and purchase more minutes. I like phone cards because if I'm out of town or at someone's house, I can make long distance calls and not have to worry about the bill being charged to the people I'm staying with.

Another way to lower your monthly bill is to cancel your cellular phone service if you're not under a contract with a company. If you are under a contract with your service provider, than stick to the guidelines of your contract and don't use more time than you're contracted for. Each additional minute can cost you 25 cents or more so be responsible when using this form of service. Some people are saying that they can't live without a cellular phone. Well, my question to them is, "How did they live without a cell phone ten years ago when only the wealthier class could afford them?"

I know that some of these suggestions may not be popular ones, but they are only for a short period of time. After your finances get back in order, you may be able to resume your normal lifestyle. If you aren't willing to make some sacrifices now while there still may be hope, than what may be a temporary financial setback, will become a permanent situation.

Another way to reduce your expenses painlessly, is to disconnect your computer online service. Now this isn't as bad as you would think because your server doesn't want to loose you as a customer, so they will usually ask you if you would like a free month to think about it. I know in my case, I paid for my online service for only 2 months and asked the company to cancel the service. The sales person gave me a free month and when I called back at the end of the month to cancel, they gave me another month for free. Well this went on for 6 months until I insisted they disconnect my service. I don't know how long they would have continued to give me free access but they weren't in any hurry to get me off the Internet. They gave me six months of service for free. That's $23. a month multiplied by 6 mos. = $138.

Some may think that $138. in 6 months is nothing to get excited about but try to remember that it's not the big bills that will knock you down, but it's usually the little bills that drain your account without you even knowing it. It has been written that it is the little foxes that spoil the vine. This statement is very true. Watch over the little things that will rob you.

Another sure fire way to save money on your Internet service is to shop around for Internet providers. I found an Internet company that gives me a 15 meg web site along with 2 search engines and a slew of extras stuff. This company gives me unlimited access to the Internet and doesn't shut down my web site, no matter how many hits my site takes. Some other providers will shut your web site down if your site takes to many hits because it taxes out their service. I get all of what I just told you about and more for only $100. a year. That's it. Not a penny more. I'm sure there are even better deals out there but this one suits me fine. Before I found this company, I was spending around $23. a month on my online server and only getting a server. That's about $250. a year, compared to the $100. a year that I'm paying now. That's $150. a year that I'm saving that I could apply to something else. Try to remember the big picture when it comes to saving money on items and services that you can get for a fraction of the price your probably paying now. Don't forget that all of this is only a part of my budget that I'm trimming and I have sacrificed very little.

Another avenue to trimming your budget is to shop around for car insurance, homeowners insurance, and life insurance. Don't just settle for the first deal that sounds good. You could literally save hundreds and even thousands of dollars each year on your insurance. Each insurance company wants to be the only insurance company that you do business with. They don't want you to go anywhere else so they will offer you incentives to make them your only agency. They will discount 20% to 30% off of your premium a year just to keep you with them, and them only. Again, you have trimmed your budget and have forfeited nothing except the few minutes it takes to shop around through the Internet or on the phone.

Another way to trim your budget is to call your power company and ask them to average out your yearly power bill and to bill you monthly on that average. I know that when I lived in the northeastern section of the United States, my power bill would fluctuate from month to month. My bill was much lower in the Summer months than it was in the Winter months. This is obviously because I didn't need to heat my house or use as much energy in the Summer vs. the Winter. My Summer energy bills were around $30. – $40. per month while my Winter energy bills were around $270. - $325. per month. This would have drastically cramped my finances had I not prepared myself for this increase in advance. Maybe this form of budgeting your power bill would work for you.

Even now that I live in the southwestern portion of the United States, my power bill has seesawed. My energy bill is now higher in the Summer because of air conditioning, as opposed to being lower in the Winter because the weather is rather mild here during those months. All I'm saying is if you budget your energy bill through the power company, there wouldn't be any unexpected surprises when the seasons change. If by chance you happen to have paid to much to the power company through this budget, they will simply reimburse you the difference and readjust your bill. However, if you use more power than what you have paid for, than the power company will typically readjust your bill to compensate the difference or just bill you the difference. At any rate, this will help you stay on a consistent budget without faltering either way.

The next time proven remedy for reducing your budget is to clip coupons. I know it sounds like a pain in the neck but my wife and I have effectively reduced our weekly grocery bill by 40%. Given the fact that we spend $120. to $140. in any given week on our groceries, this is a $40. to $50. savings per week. That's around $200. a month or roughly $2400. a year. Think of what you could do with an extra $2400. a year. Many people could use this monthly savings to reduce their credit card bill or to pay off their auto loan faster. Remember, if you don't start trying to get out of this temporary financial setback by following these simple suggestions, than this could become a permanent situation.

It only takes a few minutes to look through the newspaper and find the "Buy One Get One Free" advertisements or the "50 cent off" coupons. Keep in mind, I'm trying to painlessly help you to reduce your monthly bills without telling you to eat rice and potatoes for the next three years. However, if you are to proud to clip coupons, than maybe the rice and potato diet is the remedy for your financial situation. Believe me, I have been on that diet, and a few months of that will humble anyone to clip coupons. A good friend once told me that you don't get rich by giving your money away. That is probably one of the most profound financial statements that I've ever heard in my life. It is very true so don't give your hard earned money away to these big grocery corporations that are designed to get as much out of you as possible. $100. is worth a lot more to you than it is to these multimillion dollar companies. $100. may make the difference between your bills being paid or you being put into collections, so clip coupons and save money.

If the above suggestions don't put your budget in a range that will allow you to pay your bills, then you will need to cut your spending in the area of the miscellaneous category. You'll need to cut the spending on the things that you enjoy. Cut back on the amount of pizza or fast food that you spend your money on. Start packing a lunch instead of buying lunch at work as much. Cut back on the amount of times you go golfing or whatever you do that costs money that you could survive without. This may seem extreme but sometimes extreme times call for extreme measures. This may seem like a harsh road to travel, but you must ask yourself, "How much do I want to get out of debt without being forced to get a second or third job?"

The Budget Worksheet

Total Monthly Income = $......

Mortgage/ Rent:	$......	1 Car Payment:	$......
Food:	$......	2 Car Payment:	$......
Phone:	$......	Visa Card:	$......
Power:	$......	Master Card:	$......
Water:	$......	Discover Card:	$......
Natural Gas:	$......	Educational Loans:	$......
Car Ins.:	$......	Child Support:	$......
Renters Ins.	$......	Miscellaneous:	$......
Life Ins:	$......	....	$......
Gasoline:	$......	....	$......
Cell Phone:	$......	....	$......
Donations/ Tithe:	$......	....	$......
Pest Control:	$......	....	$......

Total Expenses Per Month = $......

Now deduct the total monthly expenses from the total monthly income. This will tell you how much money you have left over at the end of every month. If your total monthly expenses exceed your total monthly income, then you are living beyond your means and have to adjust your spending or get an additional job. If this formula shows an excess of money but you don't have the money nor can you account for it, than you are spending money unwisely someplace else.

The Killer- Credit Card Debt

I have counseled many couples about their credit situation and the one problem that surfaces 99 out of 100 times is the credit card dilemma. More couples fight about the credit cards than about any other debt they have. This is usually the worst and most crippling financial trap because it is so easy to fall into. It's easy to see something at a store like a big screen TV or a DVD player and justify owning it by simply rationalizing in your mind, that it will only cost you $30. a month. Most people don't realize that this purchase will be paid on for at least 4 years. After a month or so when the excitement of owning this new toy that you just had to have, is gone, you will still have roughly 4 years or 48 months worth of payments left. Now multiply this by 20 or 30 purchases and you are buried alive in credit card debt.

It is not uncommon for me to counsel people who have literally $30,000. to $40,000. in credit card debt and have virtually nothing to show for it except a broken big screen TV or a DVD player that they just had to have. Although this may seem funny, it is a very serious problem. When asked where the purchased product is, many reply that they don't know or they sold it at a garage sale a year after buying it. Most do not realize they have three year's left to pay on that purchase.

After helping people in this situation to get on a budget and to reconstruct their finances, they realize that this is going to take much longer to get out of this trouble than it took to get into. I have met people who feel the only way to get out of financial trouble is to file bankruptcy. This is a plan that I personally feel is the biggest mistake

11

anyone could make in their live. It's just as easy to jump out of a window and break both of your legs. The initial act isn't as painful or humiliating as the long term result. Usually, bankruptcy doesn't totally eliminate your debt. Typically, you are responsible for 10 cents on every dollar that you owe. That means if you owe $100,000. to your creditors, than you will still be responsible for paying them $10,000. If you don't file properly, than you could be in a heap of trouble and your attorney who is working for you isn't going to fix your problem that he helped you get into. You won't have any money left to sue him and he knows it. Note that Chapter 7 bankruptcy usually dissolves all of your outstanding debt while Chapter 13 bankruptcy typically allows you to pay back your creditors without paying them interest on the outstanding balances.

Another reason why not to file bankruptcy is because your financial record,(TRW), will be totally destroyed for the next 7 to 10 years. Also, your name is usually printed in the newspaper telling everybody your bankrupt, and if your from a small city or town, they will NEVER forget. Don't file bankruptcy!!!!! People with a conscience who do file, most always regret doing it.

Credit cards can vary in interest rates. These rates can range from anywhere around 3% to 21% or more depending the company you are dealing with. This means if you have a credit card with an interest rate of 21% and you owe $1,000. on that card, you will pay roughly $210. a year in interest alone. The monthly payment will typically be around $20. per $1,000. a month which means that after 12 months, you will have paid $240. to the lender but you have accrued $210. in interest for that year. This means, that out of the $240. you have paid to the credit company, only $30. will actually be put toward the amount owed. At this rate, your $1,000. purchase will be paid off in around 25-30 years. That television that was on sale for $1,000. will cost you roughly $7,200. This may seem hard to believe but see for yourself. Look at your monthly statement and check out how much your amount owed went down from payment to payment. Then multiply how many payments you have left. I can promise you that you're going to be disgusted.

I once had a consolidated loan, when I was younger and didn't know better, that had an interest rate of 25%. The amount borrowed was $5,000. and the payment was $100. a month. After a year I noticed that my payment hadn't been reduced like the lending association had said it would. When I called the lender, he told me that I had paid off about $50. of the total amount loaned to me. When I asked him what happened to the other $1,150. I had paid them, he told me that it all went to the interest on the loan. This meant that at this rate, my $5,000. loan would cost me between $50,000. to $55,000. and would take me 40 years to pay off. I thought he was joking when he gave me these figures but he assured me that this was no joke. I felt like I was doing business with a loan shark but this was all legal and there was no easy way out. However, I did get out of a loan like this and will explain how you can too. Pay close attention.

I was offered, by a credit card company, a card that had no yearly fee and had an interest rate of 5%. The low introductory rate would last for 6 months and would be raised to 19% thereafter. I accepted the offer and transferred my consolidated loan to this new card immediately. The savings was 20% or $1,000. per year in interest payments. Shortly after transferring this amount, several other credit card companies offered me the same deal as they contended for my business. I saved these applications until I was 4-5 months into my new loan and than I sent in and accepted another card from another company. As soon as my 5% rate was going to go to 19%, I would transfer the amount owed to the new card I had just received, and cancel the card I had been using. The new balance was about $4,475. I continued this pattern, using different credit cards and transferring balances from card to card for 2 years.

Finally, I called the company I was doing business at the time with and told them I wanted to cancel my credit card. When the company representative asked me why I wanted to cancel the account, I told them I had been offered a lower rate from another company. The teller then asked me if I would consider staying with the present company if they could match the rate I had been offered by another company. I agreed, and was given a fixed rate of 7%. I have long since paid off this credit card loan and haven't been in credit card debt since.

Some people literally live on their credit cards from month to month, meaning they buy everything from gasoline to groceries and charge these purchases to their credit card. At the end of every month they simply write one check for the amount they charged that month, and their bills are paid. I usually discourage this behavior because you must be very discipline in paying off your card from month to month. It's also very easy to spend more using your card than when writing a check and deducting it from your check book. Paying with a check or with cash becomes a mental exercise and keeps you more in touch with reality than when paying with plastic. If you follow the simple plan I have showed you, concerning transferring from high rates to low rates, than you will be on your way to being debt free.

Another way to pay off your credit card debt is to increase your monthly payment. This will put more money toward the principal portion and lower your payment considerably. It's a good rule of thumb to round your payment up to the nearest $10. For example; If your minimum payment is $83., than you should pay $90. Having the extra $7. in your pocket won't change your life but paying off your credit cards and getting out of debt, will.

Living debt free is easy if you discipline yourself not to use your credit cards irresponsibly. That item that you've just got to have will still be there the next time you go to the store. Weigh out every purchase and ask yourself if you really need that item, or is there something else you could use? Stop the wasteful spending and get on track so you don't have to suffer at the hands of ruthless taskmasters called creditors.

Some people have equity in their house, meaning they own a percentage of their house. This can be an advantage to them when wanting to pay off debt. If your house is worth $100,000. and you owe $75,000. on your house than this means that you have $25,000. worth of equity in your home. If your interest rate is 08% on that loan, then it would be wise to get a home equity loan against your home and pay off your credit cards that are costing you 13% - 20%. Your mortgage won't go up that much and with your credit card or auto loans paid off, you can apply the amount you were paying on them to your mortgage. If you continue to do this faithfully and not quit, you will find your mortgage is paid off faster than if you didn't apply anything and just spent the extra money you will have.

Paying Off Your House Made Easy

I've counseled countless people on the art of paying off their mortgage much faster without having to increase the mortgage payment. This is a plan that if followed, will help you retire much wealthier than you could imagine.

The average time on a mortgage is about 30 years. If the borrower, that's you, makes the payments according to the schedule set by the lender, that's the bank, then you will own your house in 30 years. If by chance you miss a payment or are late on a few payments as a result of being laid off or due to sickness, you will by penalized with fines that could be equivalent to 5 years worth of payments or more, along with damaging your credit report. You need to know that at the end of the 30 year mortgage agreement, the bank wants all of the money you owe them. If you can't get the money, they can foreclose on your home and you can loose it.

When you purchase a house for, let's say, $150,000. at an interest rate of around 7% a year, your monthly payment will be about $1,000. a month, not including insurance or taxes. After your first payment of $1000., you will have paid off about $25. in principal toward your house while the other $975. went directly to the interest. Sure you can write off your loan interest at the end of the year, but I would rather pay taxes on the money I save, than to have no money to pay tax on. At this rate, after 30 years you would have paid about $375,000. for a $150,000. house.

I'm going to show you a plan that will pay off your house in 22 years and help you retire with a substantial amount of money. You must stay on this schedule or you won't accomplish what this plan is designed to accomplish.

Let's say you have the same $150,000. mortgage along with the 7% interest rate over a 30 year period along with the same $1,000. monthly payment. You need to know the interest accrued on that loan, grows faster at the second part of the month than at the first 2 weeks of the month. If your monthly payment is due on the first day of the month, than you need to make one half payment on the middle of the month and then the other half of the payment on the first of the month. Stay 2 weeks ahead of your payment. For example: On the 1st of the month, make your $1,000. payment to get started. On the 15th of the month, make a $500. payment and write in the memo line, "Principal Only". Then, on the 1st of the month, make a $500. payment. On the 15th a $500. payment and write "Principal Only" in the memo line. On the 1st a $500. payment, and so on. Because you will be making 26 bi-weekly payments in a year, you will in fact have made 13 months worth of payments for that year. This means that an extra month's payment went to your principal and it didn't cost you anything.

Don't worry about how this equation works, it just does. Continue this process and you will pay off your house in around 22 years. It's most important to make sure you write "Principal Only" on your mid monthly check, in the memo area. If this isn't written on the check, then the $500. will not be added to the principal but will be put into an account that is paid toward your mortgage at the first of the month. Make sure you call your bank and let them know what you are doing so the bank doesn't try to play dumb and act like they don't know what's going on. Also, discuss the amounts your sending to the bank and make sure the interest on your loan is covered.

When I started making these payments, the bank conveniently didn't add this amount to the principal even though I had told them about it. The bank doesn't want you to pay off your loan faster than expected because they don't make the same money off of you as when you stay on the schedule they planned for you. Sometimes banks can't keep up with the paperwork that these transactions can take, so many banks have a plan set up to accomplish the same goal and they will most likely introduce you to it. Their scheduled plan may cost a few hundred dollars to start but it's well worth the money.

Note, that after 6 months or so the bank may try to get you back on the 30 year plan by letting you skip a month's payment. Don't skip that payment or all you have worked for in the last 6 months toward paying off your mortgage will have been for nothing. Remember, they take that skipped payment out of your principal.

Personally, I have always added an extra $100. a month to the principal of my mortgage. I know that it's just like making an extra payment a year and I desperately wanted to pay off my mortgage. How badly do you want to pay off yours? If you can afford to send in an extra $20., $50., $100., or more each month, I highly advise you do so.

Ok, so you stay on this payment plan for 22 years and you now own your house. Now you have $1,000. a month to do what ever you want with. Instead of blowing the money on a new car or a new toy of some kind, you should continue making that $1,000. payment, but not to a bank. Instead, you make the payment to an IRA,(Individual Retirement Account) for instance, or an investment fund that is indexed to the Standard & Poor's 500, commonly referred to as the S&P 500.

The S&P 500 is a category consisting of the top 500 blue chip stocks in the Dow Jones industrial average. Call a "Full Service Discount Broker" and have them establish an account for you. You can find them on the web or in a phone book. The cost is minimal and the S&P 500 has earned an average of between 12% and 13% in the last 25 years. Also, you will instantly have a diversified stock portfolio.

If you have a computer and are on the web, go to the personal finance icon and click it. There should be a number of online trading companies that will contend for your business. You can trade stocks by yourself and eliminate a brokerage firm all together, saving you even more money. The stock symbol for the fund that is indexed to the S&P 500 is "SPY". This fund is referred to as "Spiders", or "SPDRs".

There are other funds that can earn between 20% and 30% per year but you must remember, the higher the return, the higher the risk. If you make between 12% and 13% per year, then at the end of the 30 years that your mortgage was to be paid off in, you would have paid about $96,000. into your stock portfolio. This would have earned an approximate interest amount of about $60,000. and that's being very conservative. Add the $96,000 that you've contributed in the past 8 years, to the $60,000 in interest you've made and you should have approximately $156,000. in your portfolio. A more aggressive fund could literally triple this amount, earning around $150,000. to $180,000. This could give you an estimated $260,000. to help supplement your retirement.

Let's just look at your options. You could make the payments that the bank gives you, and own your house in 30 years. Or you could follow this simple plan and after 30 years, own your home and have roughly $160,000. to retire on or treat yourself to a lot of fun stuff. Remember that the $160,000 will continue to earn interest for as long as you leave it in there. 12% of $160,000 is $19,200 per year in interest. The only problem with making an extra $19,200. is having to pay the taxes on it at the end of the year. That's a far better problem than not having any money to pay tax on.

It doesn't take a financial wizard to see the position that is right for you. This is how some wealthy people get wealthy and stay wealthy. My philosophy is this, "There are to many millionaires in this world for me not to be one, and so should you." Besides, in 30 years or so, you may need that extra money just to take care of yourself due to inflation. Who will take care of you if you didn't prepare and take care of yourself or plan for your future? I hope your not relying on the government or you will die poor. It's not a sin to be poor, it's just very inconvenient. I personally followed this plan and reduced my 15 year mortgage by nearly half.

My situation was a little different because when I paid off my credit cards, I just shifted the amount I paid on the cards to the principal of my mortgage. This reduced my mortgage significantly. I would encourage you to do the same. In the end, the feeling of financial freedom is unparalleled. Right now, your probably thinking that it must be nice to be in these shoes, but you can change the path your on right now by following this simple plan.

Another way to pay off your mortgage is to simply make an extra mortgage payment at the end of each year. Use your tax return or whatever extra money you may have to make this payment. Remember, if you make an extra payment each year towards your principal, that reduces your mortgage by 2 to 3 months the first year.

This number increases the closer you get toward the end of your mortgage. I personally don't push this idea because most of us don't have an extra $1,000. to throw towards our mortgage payment. Most of us would rather treat ourselves to something nice. Keep in mind that your mortgage is a long term loan so think of it as a marathon, not the 100 yard dash. If you treat it like the 100 yard dash, you'll loose your steam and motivation quickly and burn out of the race. Look at it as though you have the next 22 years to finish this race, so pace yourself and stay 100 yards ahead of the banks. The 100 yard dash is compared to your credit card bills, or auto and boat payments. Pay those off as soon as possible and with all of the energy you have.

Andrew J. Green

Generating Income

The average American has over $1,000. worth of articles in their house or garage that they regard as garbage. Old golf clubs, bikes, coin and stamp collections, radios, pictures, antique furniture, fishing poles and gear, guns, tables and chairs, extra televisions and camping equipment, old chainsaws and lawn equipment, power saws and tools, you name it, and most people will usually say that it's not worth the time nor the effort to get anything for it. Many people will say that they can't live without a certain item even though the item has been buried in the closet for the past ten years.

This stuff may stand between you paying off your debt or you filing bankruptcy. Do you really need it or is it something that is just taking up space and would be better off in somebody else's garage? I personally went through my house and garage and looked for something that I could sell. I put out all of my old army fatigues, and things I regarded as garbage or junk. From old lamps that don't match the decor, to an old wagon that I towed behind my lawn tractor. While on this quest, I found $60. in loose pennies, nickels and dimes that were laying around in my house.

After selling all of the junk I had acquired in the last few years or so, I generated $1,200. That's $1,200. worth of garage sale junk that was cluttering up my home. That's $1,200. that was not being used to reduce my debt. After the initial shock of the $1,200. had worn off, I decided to call the junk yard and see how much they would give me for my old rusted pick up truck with a blown engine. They towed it away and gave me $50. So I had received $1,250. for all of my junk along with finding $60. in pennies, nickels, and dimes. If someone

21

had told me I had this much money laying around my home, I would have told them they needed their head examined. Well, I'm telling you that you have articles that could be turned into money in your very own home.

You are probably thinking that this guy is crazy, but I challenge you to look around your home and whatever you find that you think is worthless, that's what will probably bring in a dollar or two. Multiply this by 100 of these worthless things, and that's a couple hundred dollars you just generated. How many hammers do you have? How many hammers do you need? If when your going through your home, and you don't find anything you can get rid of, than ask yourself when the last time you used these things. If you haven't used this thing in the last six months, then you don't need it. If these are seasonal items such as snow blowers or lawn mowers, then don't include these in your list, but just about everything else can go. Note, that whatever you don't sell, you can give to charities and with the receipt they give you, you can write the donation off at tax time. Remember, you just want to generate money to reduce your debt. After reducing your debt, you can always repurchase these "Things" when you are out of financial straits. If you refuse to get rid of anything, then ask yourself, "How bad do I really want to get out of debt?" Then make the decision.

The American Way

I have encountered people, who after reviewing their finances and debts, the only way to reduce their debt and stay afloat, is to get a better paying job. To most, this is a fate worse than death. Their credit is shot yet they want to retire wealthy. In other words, they want to have their cake and eat it too. In short, they want it the American way.

I have met people who have an insurmountable debt problem due to either irresponsibility or just through bad fortune. Through bad investments, divorce, or the death of a family member, which can leave someone in a terrible position. These unfortunate people, for whom my heart breaks, find no mercy from the creditors who swoop down like vultures on a fresh kill.

Fortunately for these people, the system is on their side. In this great country of The United States Of America, there is very little that creditors will do to you, in most cases, as long as you make an honest effort to pay your debt. For example: If you make arrangements with each creditor to make payments of $20. per month, then they usually won't send you to collections. However, if you are put into collections, the collectors will help make arrangements with you and will generally accept what you can afford. This rule may be different concerning auto loans and real estate, but with hospital bills, doctor bills, and credit cards, these rules generally apply. This means that if you owe $100,000. in medical expenses to 5 different doctors or hospitals, your monthly payment to them collectively will be $100. per month. The key to this is to call all of the creditors and tell them what is happening and arrange payments that are comfortable for you.

Then they know that you are doing your best and not trying to evade their notices.

I strongly suggest you call the Consumer Credit Counseling office near you and find out what the laws are in your state concerning good faith payments to creditors. It's also wise to ask your county recorder about Homesteading your house so your creditors can't take it away from you, ever! Note that Homesteading is in no way filing bankruptcy and doesn't hurt your credit. Homesteading should be filed immediately after purchasing your home and prior to having credit problems. Filing after you have creditors all over you may be to late and may not help you.

Let's say for example you owe $40,000. to 8 different credit card companies. This is costing you around $800. a month. You owe 5 different doctors $100,000. collectively. The doctors will want this amount paid off within 6 months. You know you will never be able to pay them in this short amount of time. The vultures are now hovering over head and you feel like you are suffocating, but there is nothing you think you can do about it. Your car payments are $400. each and you have 2 cars. The mortgage is $1,000. a month along with general living expenses like food, insurance, power, phone, and everything else. Your total monthly bills are around $4,000.

The first move I advise people to make is to call their creditors. The worst mistake that people make is not contacting their creditors. For some reason, consumers think that if they don't contact the creditor, than the creditor will go away. Remember the Golden Rule in this situation. It's, "He who has the gold rules." You, the consumer, have the gold. The creditor wants to get the gold from you. So in a sense, you can dictate to them what's going to take place, within reason. Try to work out a payment plan that is extremely comfortable for you. A plan that will leave you with a lot of money at the end of the month. Remember, they are a business. All they want to do is get their money, not your first born child. But they will take everything if you let them bully you into it.

After setting up your payment plan, you should make sure you have at least $500. a month left over that is not going to the creditors any longer, because you told them you couldn't pay it. This $500. you invest wisely. Call a full service discount broker and invest that $500 per month into a stock fund that will average 12% - 13% per year.

$500. a month equals $6,000. a year. In 10 years, with interest included, there will be roughly $121,355. in your account. That $121,355. will be doubling every 6 years or so. If you didn't contribute any more money, than in 10 more years, when you are 60 or 70 years old, you would have $390,000. That $390,000 will be doubling every 6 years. That's about $65,000. in interest a year that can supplement your income.

I use this as a worst case example but many people reading this book may be in this position. Know that your not alone. In my state, 6 out of every 10 people have filed bankruptcy. This is a position you don't want to be in. If you can't get control of your finances now, what makes you think you will learn when your bankrupt? You won't. Most of the people that I know who have filed bankruptcy are in financial trouble within 3 to 4 years after filing. They've learned nothing except how to be irresponsible and how to get buried back up their eyes in debt with no way out. Some people tell me they plan to just file again when they've milked the system for everything its worth, not knowing they can't file for at least 4 to 7 years, depending on their situation. I guess that's just their way of thinking though.

Andrew J. Green

Earning It Vs. Making It

I often hear people say to me how last week at work, they "made" so much money and this week they will "make" so much money. Well this type of statement couldn't be further from the truth. Actually, these people didn't "make" any money at all, they "earned" it. "Making" money and "earning" money are two totally different acts but have the same outcome. That outcome is that money is put into your pocket. Personally, I would rather "make" money than "earn" it and I would venture to say, so would you.

When you go to work and grind out a paycheck every week, you are "earning" that money, as opposed to having someone or something "make" money for you. When you "earn" a paycheck in any given week, you have "made" money for the company you work for. If you invested your money in the stock market for example, and that investment "earns" $50., then you have just "made" $50. Minimal effort was exerted by you personally because your money is now working for you instead of you working for your money.

To me, dollar bills are like a work force of faithful, loyal employees. When I put my dollar bill work force to work for me, they never call in sick, never ask for a raise, never need a vacation, do exactly what I tell them to do, and they work 24 hours a day, 7 days a week, 365 days a year.

If you follow the simple instructions of this book, you should end up having a work force of employees like the one I just described. These employees will do everything you tell them to do when you put them to work for you as long as you don't let them sit around.

27

If you put them to work for you in a CD (Certificate of Deposit) at an interest rate of 3% for example, then they will not let you down. They will "earn" you exactly 3% a year for as long as the terms of that CD are. If you put that work force to work for you in a stock portfolio that will "earn" you 20% a year or 20% a day, then that is what your dollars will do for you. This is how people who are rich, stay rich and don't work very hard for their money. The only difficult part of this plan is knowing where to put your work force to work for you.

Every stock broker or entrepreneur trying to generate money will tell you to invest your money in them or their product because, "It's a chance of a lifetime". This "line" is compared to a guy saying to a girl, "What's a girl like you doing in a place like this?" It's the oldest and worst pick up line around, but people still use it anyway. You wouldn't believe how many "chances of a lifetime", I have brushed off and those "chances of a lifetime" lost the money of everyone that invested in them. There will be "chances of a lifetime" everyday of the week.

Everyday, there are paupers who become millionaires as a result of their investing and everyday there are millionaires who become paupers as a result of their investments. You must ask yourself how much you are willing to wager on an investment. Are the rewards worth taking the chance of loosing your money? Ask yourself what you could buy with that $1,000. you want to invest. That $1,000. could buy you gasoline for your car for 6 months or so. It could pay for groceries for the next 10 weeks. You could even treat yourself to something you have had your eye on for a while.

Now you must ask yourself what might happen if you don't invest that $1,000. in something that might "make" you another $1,000. It's as though you lost $1,000. that you may have "made" if you had invested it. This decision is entirely up to you but you need to know that if you never attempt to "make" money, then I can almost guarantee you that you will surely "earn" every dollar you ever get. Unless of course your rich uncle dies and leaves you ten million dollars. I don't know about you, but I'm not holding my breath for that.

Your future is in your hands. What are you going to do to prepare for it. You had better do something soon because if your 20 years old today, your going to be 50 years old tomorrow and when you look in the mirror, what will you see? A person who held on to $1,000. for 30 years and has nothing to show for it? Or the person who invested $1,000. 30 years ago and "made" 10% a year and now has $17,440. to supplement his or her income?

Many people don't realize this but a $100. bill invested today in an account that "earns" 10% per year, will "earn" $1,744. in 30 years. Now figure out how many $100. bills we as Americans burn up on miscellaneous things that we could probably do without. Then multiply all of those $100. bills wasted in one year by 10%, every year for 30 years. This number could be well over $100,000.

Most people don't realize this but that same $100 bill invested today in an account that "earns" 20% per year for 30 years, will "earn" $23,737. in 30 years. 10% gives you $1,744. while 20% gives you $23,737. over the same period of time. The only problem with trying to get the 20% is that you'll most likely loose a lot of your money with the riskier investments needed to generate this kind of return, but it is possible. The whole point is that you need to have that $100. bill to make any investment. Think of the potential your money could have if you don't blow it foolishly.

When your 65 or 70 years old, you won't remember how good that hamburger or soda tasted. You won't remember how much fun you had with the item that you just had to have. You won't remember all of the rounds you bought for your friends at the local bar or how many lunches you bought for your friends at work. But what you will remember will be how you squandered away what you had that may have helped you in your later years.

I'm not saying that you shouldn't have fun and enjoy your life while your young. I'm not at all saying that you should live to support yourself when you are older. But what I am saying is that you are going to answer to someone as to what you did with the finances that you have received in your life. Are you going to be calling yourself a fool because of how you have acted in the past? As an older person, are you going to have to pay for your foolish choices or are you going to look in the mirror as a wealthy older person and say you have done well.? Hopefully, you will be grateful for the wisdom you gleaned along in life off of different people who have been put in your path to help you along the way. I hope you are not the person with many regrets. But if you are, than only you will have to look in the mirror and answer to the one looking back at you as to why your in the shoes your in. Don't live for the future, but plan for it.

The Rule Of 72

This may very well be one of the shortest chapters you will ever read, but I assure you it may also be one of the most informative. When investing, if you want to know how long it will take for your investment to double, you need to know, "The Rule Of 72". Divide 72 by the average amount of interest you are receiving on your investment. The answer you come up with will be the amount of years it will take for your investment to double. For example: If you are receiving 9 % a year on an investment, then 72 divided by 9 % = 8 years. Your investment will earn a 100% return in 8 years as long as it averages 9 % for 8 consecutive years.

Another example: If you receive 20 % a year on your investment, then 72 / 20 % = 3.6 years. Your investment will double in 3.6 years as long as it averages 20 % a year for 3.6 years.

Last example: If your investment earns 4 % a year, then 72 / 4 = 18 years. You will double your money in 18 years as long as you average 4 % a year for 18 years.

Andrew J. Green

Pigs Get Fat - Hogs Get Slaughtered

The name of this chapter is symbolic of money minded people who gradually work their way to financial success vs. greedy people who try to get everything all at once. Becoming financially secure doesn't happen over night. People who play the roll of a Hog will usually get slaughtered by their own greed. They are fools who make money their god. They will take everything you have without considering you, even though they already have much. These types of people try to be deep thinkers but are usually shallow minded. They will probably die with millions of dollars but don't have a friend or loved one in the world. The reason for this is typically because they have sold their loved ones and friends down the road somewhere. I've met a number of people like this. One such person grew up in a family whose name is synonymous with money and whose families money helped build America. He was married 6 times and divorced 6 times. He had many children but they mostly hate him. His money and success drew him away from everything that was once precious to him. He believed that his divorces cost him everything. He eventually he put a gun in his mouth and ended his life.

In his suicide letter he wrote that he had nothing to live for because he has lost everything. He wrote that he felt poor and how he was on the brink of homelessness. His letter continued telling of his poverty and how he justified taking his own life. He wrote how he must end his life for the sole reason that he had become a pauper because he only had ten million dollars left to his name. That is not a misprint. He died with ten million dollars to his name. This man was slaughtered by his own mind-sets and by the system he lived in.

Is this the life you would want? Hogs usually get everything quickly, if they succeed, and don't appreciate it as much as you or I would. Hogs typically don't have money, money has them. They're prisoners in a cell that has invisible bars. They think their free but they are trapped and lost in a maze that continues to change.

One of the wealthiest men that ever lived was asked how much money was going to be enough for him. His reply was, "Just a few more dollars." People like him will never get enough. Their soul is empty and they are trying to fill it with things that money can buy.

How much is enough for you? Will you get out of the bondage of debt, only to become a slave of money? Will you become a Pig who gets fat and healthy and has more than enough, or will you become a Hog, who can't get enough even if he owns the world? Ask yourself, "How much will be enough?" Write your answer on a piece of paper. File it in a place where you can read it when you succeed and see if you've changed your views.

Here is a piece of advice. If you invest in a stock or anything, and you make 10% when you sell it, if that stock goes up $1,000. after you have sold it, don't look at it as though you lost $1,000. because you sold to early. That stock could have just as easily gone the other way and you would have lost if you had still owned it. People who think this way are of the Hog mind-set. Just be satisfied you made 10% and didn't loose it.

The Game A Base Hit Or A Home Run

Financial investing in the stock market or in collectable cards is just like a baseball game. You can get a base hit, strike out, or hit a home run. You can drop the ball costing you a run, or catch a fly ball and win the game. The only way you will ever know how well you will do is if you get into the game.

Many people I counsel are constantly looking for that home run investment. Everyone wants to hit a home run in the area of finances. But financial games, like baseball games, aren't won by hitting home runs. They're won by getting base hits. Everyone is looking for that perfect pitch. For example: How many people do you know who wouldn't have invested in Microsoft Computer 15 years ago if they knew what the outcome would have been? Or who wouldn't have invested in AOL, Dell Computer, Amazon, or any other home run investment? You probably don't know many people who wouldn't have bought stock in these companies. But while people are looking for that perfect investment, they are passing up on base hits which are costing them the game. Let me save you some time and say there are no perfect investments along with no guarantees that your investment won't become a total looser. But there are ways to get on base which gives you a better chance of making a run. For example: I purchased a stock I had been watching for a month. The stock kept dropping to around $9. and would rise to $11. or $12. within a couple of days or so. This may seem to be only a couple dollars but keep in mind that this is 20% to 30% of the stock value. Within 8 weeks I had doubled my investment by just getting those $2. or $3. base hits. When the price went down, I bought. As soon as it went up 20%, I sold. I only had to do this 5 times or so and this would be equivalent to hitting a home run and making 100%. Don't look for a home run while the base hits are passing you by.

People are constantly asking me what to invest in. My reply is simply, "Buy what you know". If you know antiques, than buy antiques at garage sales or wherever and sell them for a profit. If you know the value of collectibles, than buy and sell them to other collectors.

A couple years ago a man asked me to buy his shotgun for $100. I knew I could sell the gun for more than $100. without even trying just by his description of the gun. I purchased the gun and the man was happy with the deal. Two days later I sold the gun for $750. to a collector. I bought and sold what I knew about. This has happened a number of times to me because I know the value of certain items.

Now ask yourself, "What do I know about?" What gold mine of knowledge do you have hidden within your head? Everybody knows something. You can go to your local bookstore and find books on the values of just about anything. The same idea goes generally with buying stocks. Buy what you know and like. For example: What stores do you shop at? Chances are they may be on the stock exchange. What clothes do you wear and like? What shoes do you like? Who makes these products? If the product is good than there is a good chance the stock will do well. I use to ask my teenage children what is in style amongst their crowd. Stores that high school kids shop at are like gold mines for the owners of the stock.

Stock brokers don't have a crystal ball, so don't expect them to have any sure fire ideas. Most brokers I know are broker than anyone. All they usually tell me is how much they lost last week. They get paid a commission weather you make money off of their advice or not. Buy what you know!

Money is being made everywhere, from bottle caps to model planes. From canoes to furniture. The game is being played. You can either be a bystander in the crowd or a player in the game. Time is ticking away and it's your turn to bat. Don't wait around, get into the game. Get out of debt and get into the game.

About the Author

Andrew Green was born in central New York State and lived there for most of his life. He attended college and majored in Business Law and Economics. He has been counseling on finance for 10 years and has helped some of the most hopeless financial cases get turned around onto a successful road. He holds back no financial secrets and uses the simple steps in this book to solve the problems people have concerning their finances.

Andrew now lives in the desert southwestern section of the United States with his precious wife and two children. He is helping people construct and reconstruct their business and personal lives everyday.

Printed in the United States
24544LVS00006B/331-333